The Drummer Boy
from Maine

THE AUTHOR LATER IN LIFE

The Drummer Boy from Maine

With Company H, 8th Maine Volunteers in the American Civil War

George T. Ulmer

LEONAUR

The Drummer Boy from Maine: With Company H,
8th Maine Volunteers in the American Civil War
by George T. Ulmer

Leonaur is an imprint of Oakpast Ltd

Material original to this edition and presentation of the
text in this form copyright © 2011 Oakpast Ltd

ISBN: 978-0-85706-625-1 (hardcover)
ISBN: 978-0-85706-626-8 (softcover)

http://www.leonaur.com

Publisher's Notes

Contents

Dedicated to the
Grand Army of the Republic

Preface

In submitting this little book the author does not attempt to edit a history of the rebellion, nor does he assume to be correct in the date of events to a day. He does not hope or expect to make a hero of himself by writing it, for he was far from doing anything heroic, believing, as he does, that most of the heroes of the war were killed. Perhaps the *writing* of this book may stamp him a hero, and for his audacity in so doing some one may kill him. But he intends to clothe his little work in homely, rugged, commonplace language. Not striving to make it a work of literary merit, only a truthful account of an unimportant career and experience in the army. It may, perhaps, be interesting to some of his comrades, who recollect the incidents or recall similar events that happened to themselves, and thereby serve the purpose of introducing one of the youngest soldiers and a comrade of that greatest and most noble of all organizations, the Grand Army of the Republic.

Respectfully,

George T. Ulmer

The Bombardment of Fort Sumter

ombardment of Fort Sumter. This was the beginning and the first sound of actual war which inspired me, and kindled the fire of patriotism in my youthful breast. The little spark lay smouldering for two long years, 'till at last it burst forth into a full blaze. When Fort Sumter was bombarded, I was a midget of a boy; a barefooted, ragged newsboy in the city of New York. The bombardment was threatened for several weeks before it actually occurred; and many nights I would have been bankrupted, but that everyone was on the *qui vive* for the event, and I got myself into lots of trouble by shouting occasionally, "Fort Sumter Bombarded!" I needed money; it sold my papers, and I forgave myself. When the authentic news did come, I think it stirred up within me as big a piece of fighting desire as it did in larger and older people. I mourned the fact that I was then too small to fight, but lived in hopes that the war would last until I should grow. If I could have gone south, I felt that I could have conquered the rebellious faction alone, so confident was I of my fighting abilities.

In the fall of '61 my dear mother died, and my father who had a great desire to make possibilities out of improbabilities, and believing a farm the proper place to bring up a family of boys, bought one away in the interior of Maine. The farm was very hilly, covered with huge pines and liberally planted with granite ledges. I used to think God wanted to be generous to this state and gave it so much land it had to be stood up edgeways. Picture to yourself, dear reader, four boys taken from the busy life of a great city, place them in the wilderness of Maine, where they had to make a windrow of the forest to secure a garden spot for the house, pry out the stumps and blast the ledges to sow the seed, then ask yourself what should the harvest be?

Father's business required all of his time in New York City, and we were left with two hired men to develop the farm, our brains and muscles, but mine didn't seem to develop worth a cent. I didn't care for the farmer's life. The plough and scythe had no charms for me. My horny, hardened little hand itched and longed to beat the drums that would marshal men to arms.

After eight months of hard work we had cleared up quite a respectable little farm, an oasis in that forest of pines. A new house and barn had been built, also new fences and stone walls, but not much credit for this belonged to me. Soon after, we received a letter from father stating that he would be with us in a short time and bring us a new mother and a little step-sister. This was joyous news, the anticipation of a new mother, and above all a step-sister, inspired us with new ambition. The fences and barn received a coat of whitewash, the stones were picked out of the road in front of the house, the wood-pile was re-piled and everything put into apple-pie order. We did not know what day they would arrive. So each day about the time the stage coach from Belfast should pass the corners, we would perch ourselves on the fence in front of the house to watch for it, and when it did come in sight, wonder if the folks were in it; if they were, it would turn at the corners and come toward our house. Day after day passed, and they did not come, and we had kind of forgotten about it. Finally one day while we were all busy burning brush, brother Charlie came rushing towards us shouting, "The stage coach is coming! The stage is coming!" Well, such a scampering for the house! We didn't have time to wash or fix up, and our appearance would certainly not inspire our city visitors with much paternal pride or affection; we looked like charcoal burners. Our faces, hands and clothes were black and begrimed from the burning brush, but we couldn't help it; we were obliged to receive and welcome them as we were. I pulled

The Memorable Bombardment of Fort Sumter

up a handful of grass and tried to wipe my face, but the grass being wet, it left streaks all over it, and I looked more like a bogie man than anything else. We all struggled to brush up and smooth our hair, but it was no use, the stage coach was upon us, the door opened, father jumped out, and as we crowded around him, he looked at us in perfect amazement and with a kind of humiliated expression behind a pleasant fatherly smile he exclaimed, "Well, well, you are a nice dirty looking lot of boys. Lizzie," addressing his wife and helping her to alight, "This is our family, a little smoky; I can't tell which is which, so we'll have to wait till they get their faces washed to introduce them by their names." But our new mother was equal to the occasion for coming to each of us, and taking our dirty faces in her hands, kissed us, saying at the same time, "Philip, don't you mind, they are all nice, honest, hard-working boys, and I know I shall like them, even if this country air has turned their skins black." At this moment a tiny voice called, "Please help me out." All the boys started with a rush, each eager to embrace the little step-sister. I was there first, and in an instant, in spite of my dirty appearance, she sprang from the coach right into my arms; my brothers struggled to take her from me, but she tightened her little arms about my neck and clung to me as if I was her only protector. I started and ran with her, my brothers in full chase, down the road, over the stone walls, across the field, around the stumps with my prize, the brothers keeping up the chase till we were all completely tired out, and father compelled us to stop and bring the child to the house. Afterward we took our turns at caressing and admiring her; finally we apologized for our behaviour and dirty faces, listened to father's and mother's congratulations, concluded father's choice for a wife was a good one, and that our little step-sister was just exactly as we wanted her to be, and the prospect of a bright, new and happy home seemed to be already realized.

A home is all right
With father and brother,
But darker than night
Without sister and mother.

CHAPTER 2

Enlisted & Mustered

The war grew more and more serious. Newspapers were
eagerly sought; and every word about the struggle was read
over and over again. A new call for troops was made, another
and still another, and I was all the time fretting and chafing
in the corn or potato field, because I was so young and small.
I could not work; the fire of patriotism was burning me up.
My eldest brother had arrived at the age and required size to
fit him for the service; he enlisted and went to the front. This
added new fuel to the flame already within me, and one day I
threw down the hoe and declared that I would go to the war!
I would join my brother at all hazards. My folks laughed at me
and tried to dissuade me from so unwise a step, but my mind
was made up, and I was bound to enlist. Enlist I did, when I was
only fourteen years of age and extremely small for my years, but
I thought I would answer for a drummer boy if nothing else.
I found that up hill work, however, but I was bound to "get
there," and—I did.

It was easy enough to enlist, but to get mustered into the
service was a different thing. I tried for eight long weeks. I enlisted in my own town, but was rejected. I enlisted in an adjoin-
ing town—rejected, and so on for weeks and weeks. But I did
not give up. I owned at the time a little old gray horse and a
two-wheeled jumper or "gig," which I had bought with my
savings from the sale of "hoop poles," which are small birch and
alder trees that grow in the swamps, and used for hoops on lime
casks; at this time they were worth a half a cent a piece deliv-

ered. I would work cutting these poles at times when I could do nothing else, pack them on my back to the road, pile them up, till I had a quantity to sell. At length I concluded I had enough to buy me a horse and cart; the pile seemed as big as a house to me, but when the man came along to buy them, he counted out six thousand good ones and rejected nine thousand that were bad. "Too small!" he said.

"Too small?" I exclaimed, "why there is hardly any difference in them!" But he was buying, I was selling, and under the influence of a boy's anxiety, he paid me thirty dollars, which I counted over and over again, and at every count the dollars seemed to murmur, "A horse, a horse!—war! war! to the front! be a soldier!" I could picture nothing but a soldier's life; I could almost hear the sounds of the drums, and almost see the long rows of blue-coated soldiers marching in glorious array with steady step to the music of the band. "Thirty! thirty!" I would repeat to myself, but finally concluded thirty wouldn't buy much of a horse, but my heart was set upon it, and nothing remained for me to do but cut more "poles." One day when I arrived at the road with a bundle of them, a farmer happened to be passing, driving a yoke of oxen as I tumbled my hoop-poles over the fence on to the pile.

"Heow be yer?" Addressing me in a high, nasal twang peculiar to the yeomanry of Maine, and then calling to his oxen without a change of tone, he drawled, "Whoa! back! Whoa you, Turk! Whoa, Bright!" at the same time hitting the oxen over their noses with his goad-stick, and resting on the yoke, he asked, "What yer goin' ter dew with them poles?"

"Sell them," I replied.

"What dew yer want for 'em?" taking in the height and width of the pile with a calculating eye.

"Fifty cents a hundred," I said, with some trepidation.

"Don't want nothin', dew yer," coming over and picking out the smallest pole in the pile; "Pooty durned small, been't they? What'll yer take fur the hull lot?"

"Twenty dollars," I said.

"Twenty dollars! Whew!" Emitting a whistle that would have

done credit to a locomotive exhausting steam. "Why, thar been't more'n a thousan' thar, be thar?"

"Oh yes, I guess there are over four thousand."

"Say!" sticking his hands in either breeches pocket and taking me in from head to foot with a comprehensive glance, "What might yer name be?"

"Ulmer," I said.

"No? You been't Phil's son, be yer?"

"Yes, sir."

"Yer don't tell me! Wall, by gosh! I like Phil, he's a durned smart 'un. I'll tell yer what, I'd like ter see him and Jimmie Blaine a settin' up in them gol-durn presidential cheers; why, by gosh, they'd jist open the hull durned treasury bildin' an let all ther gorramed gold an' silver role right out inter the streets, by gosh, they would." Having delivered himself of this pane-gyric, together with an accumulated quantity of saliva resulting from the constant mastication of a large tobacco quid, he again turned his attention to the pile of poles and said, "How much did yer say fur the lot?"

"Twenty dollars."

"Twenty!" Drawing the corners of his mouth down and stroking his chin, then turning to me, "Wall, more I look at yer, by gosh, yer do look like Phil. Wall, I'd like purty well ter have them poles, but—," as if a sudden idea had struck him,—"Don't want ter trade fur a horse, dew yer?"

"What kind of a horse?"

"Wall, a pooty durned good 'un. I hain't druve him much lately, but he yused ter go like smoke; he's a leetle old but, will prick up his ears like a colt when he's a mind ter."

"Well, I do want a horse, if I can trade for one," I said, trying not to show anxiety.

"Say, got time ter get on' ter the waggin an go over to my farm and see him, take dinner with me? Guess, the old woman'll have enough for both."

Being anxious, I accepted the invitation, and was soon on the way. He pestered me with all kinds of questions; asked all about my family affairs and told me all of his and every other

family for miles about. Finally we reached his house, one of those old-fashioned farm houses with several old tumble-down sheds and out-buildings attached, near by an old barn that was once painted red, the shingles had rotted and blown off here and there, so you could see daylight from any portion inside. Scattered about were old wagon boxes, odd wheels, old toothless harrows, ploughs, a wheelbarrow upside down with the wheel gone, part of an old harness lying across it; bits of harness were hanging on pegs in the barn. Geese, turkeys and chickens were numerous and clucked about as if they were really pleased to see us, and in fact, I discounted or anticipated the looks of the house from the careless dilapidated appearance of every thing around and about the old man's farm.

He finally unyoked his oxen, dropped the yoke right where he took it off and turned his cattle into the yard. "Now then, we'll get a bite to eat, and I'll show you two horses, and durn me if I won't give you your choice and a good trade." "Martha-Ann," he called, "Martha-Ann!"

In a moment a little, bright, bustling old woman came to the door and shading her eyes with her apron, called back: "What is it, Dan'l? Did you bring the merlasses, and candles, and the broom?"

"Yes," he answered back.

"And the salt?"

"Yes."

"And the rennet for the cheese, and the salt-pork?"

"Yes, yes, yes," he answered, "and I've brought a young man, Phil. Ulmer's son; goin to trade him 'Dick.'"

"What?" said she, coming out to where we were. "Now, Dan'l, you are not going to do anything of the kind."

"Yes, I be," he said.

"You shan't, I won't have my horse sold; you know he is the only one I can drive, and he is so kind and gentle, and the only good horse you have; you shan't sell him." And then she sat down on the cart-tongue and cried as if her heart would break, and I began to think I was going to really get a splendid horse at a bargain.

All through the dinner she sobbed, and when she would pass me bread or anything, it was with a heartbroken sigh, and I began to want that horse.

Finally dinner finished, he took me to the barn. There were two horses together standing on the barn-floor eating corn-husk. They both looked as if they never had eaten anything else. One was a bay, and the other a grey; they were so poor that you could mistake either for a barrel with half the staves fallen in.

"Thar, sir, be two fine critters; you can have either; this grey one is Dick, the one the old woman is so sot on, but he's getting too frisky for her ter handle, he's the best dispositioned animal yer ever saw; yer do anything with him, he's always ready. Get him with 'tother on a load at the bottom of a big hill and he's thar every time; yer see, he's a leetle sprung in one knee thar, he done that by pulling; it don't hurt him a bit ter drive, and go! Why, do you know he's trotted in two minutes? You notice, one eye's bit off colour! Blue? Wall sir, that was strained a leetle by watching over his blinder to see that no other hoss should pass or get near him when he were druve on the race track twelve years ago, but it don't hurt him now."

"You praise this horse," I remarked, "but don't say a word about the other."

"Oh, he don't need it," said the old man dryly.

I was so anxious to get a horse, I concluded to take Dick. I thought, he must be the best on Martha-Ann's account, and really there didn't seem much choice.

"You want a harness and waggin too, don't yer?"

"Yes," I replied, "I shall have to have something to drive him in."

"Wall, I guess I can fix you out with a full rig."

So after looking through the sheds, he pulled out an old gig with one shaft broken and without wheels. "Guess I'll find the wheels of this somewhar. Do you know this is the same gig that very Dick yused ter haul on the race track; he may remember it after yer hitch him into it. If he does, you want to look out for him, and here are the wheels."

He pulled them out of a pile of old lumber and rubbish, and

fitted them on; one was badly dished in and was painted red, the other was as badly dished out and one day had been painted yellow; but I was anxious and didn't object; I wanted to get home.

So after getting the "gig" together, he patched a harness from the odd pieces he found, then fitted them on to the poor horse who looked as if he was sorry he was alive.

Finally we had everything all ready. I mounted the "gig." As I did so, I noticed it seemed one sided, and looking at the wheels, I found one was somewhat larger than the other, but said nothing. Taking up the lines made up my mind to get home and fix it there. I pulled on the reins and spoke to "Dick," but he didn't move. The old man took him by the bridle and led him to the road remarking at the same time, "Dick never did like to go away from home."

After we reached the road, the old man hit "Dick" with a hoe handle, and off he started. It was four miles from his house to ours, and I reached home *next day*. Figured up what the whole thing cost me: The horse stood me $33.50, the "gig" $7.50, and the harness 75 cents. This was my outfit to make or break me. My brothers laughed at my trade, but I didn't care, I had a purpose, and I was bound to accomplish it.

When I wanted to use my "rig" to harness the horse, I was obliged to take a ladder to put his bridle on, lead him alongside of the steps to put the saddle and breeching on, and back him up to the well-curb to put his tail in the "crupper," and after he was hitched to the "gig," nine times out of ten he would wait till he was ready to go.

Some time after I learned that uncle "Dan'l" was a regular horse dealer and kept just such old plugs around him, and that they were always his wife's favourites when the old man wanted to get one off his hands. However, Dick and I became great friends. I fixed up the old "gig," and it answered my purpose. I got there with it.

It became a customary daily routine for me to harness this poor animal, start at sundown and drive all night. Where? Why to Augusta to try and get mustered in, but I would always ride back broken hearted and disappointed, my ardour, however, not dampened a bit. I became a guy to my brothers and neighbours. My father and step-sister indulged me in my fancy, helping me all they could—father by furnishing me with money, and step-sister by putting up little lunches for my pilgrimages during the night. They thought me partially insane, and judged it would be best to let me have my own idea, with the hope that it would soon wear off. But it didn't. I would not give up. The Yankee yearning for fight had possession of me, and I could neither eat, sleep nor work. I was bound to be a soldier. I prayed for it, and I sometimes thought, my prayers were answered; that the war should last 'till I was big enough to be one—for it did.

I had enlisted four times in different towns, and each time I went before a mustering officer, I was rejected. "Too small" I was every time pronounced, but I was not discouraged or dismayed—the indomitable pluck and energy of those down east boys pervaded my system. I was bound to get there, for what I didn't know, I did not care or didn't stop to think. I only thought of the glory of being a soldier, little realizing what an absurd-looking one I would make; but the ambition was there, the pluck was there, and the patriotism of a man entered the breast of the wild dreamy boy. I wanted to go to the front—and I went.

After several unsuccessful attempts to be mustered into the service at Augusta, which was twenty-five miles from our little farm, I thought I would enlist from the town of Freedom and thereby get before a different mustering officer who was located in Belfast. I had grown, I thought, in the past six weeks, and before a new officer, I thought my chances of being accepted would improve; so on a bright morning in September I mounted my gig, behind my little old gray horse, who seemed to say, as he turned his head to look at me when I jumped on to the seat, "What a fool you are, making me haul you all that distance, when you know they won't have you!" but kissing my little step-sister good-bye, with a wave of my hand to father and brothers who stood in the yard and door of the dear old home, I drove away, and as I did so I could see the expressions of ridicule and doubt on their faces, while underneath it all there was a tinge of sadness and fear. They did not think for a moment. I would be mustered into the army, yet fear took possession of them when I drove off, for they knew my determined disposition.

Well, I arrived in Belfast. Instead of driving direct to the stable and hotel, and putting my horse up, I drove direct to the office of the mustering officer. I did not need to fasten my trusty horse, for he knew it would only be a few moments, and as I went to the office door, he turned his head and whinnied as if he were laughing at me. I entered that office like a young Napoleon. I had made up my mind to walk in before the officer very erect and dignified, even to raising myself on tiptoe. On telling the clerk my errand, he ushered me into an inner office, and imagine my surprise—my consternation—when, swinging around in his chair, I found myself in the presence of the very officer who had rejected me in Augusta so many times.

"Damn it," said he, "will you never let up? Go home to your mother, boy, don't pester me any more. I will not accept you, and let that end it."

I tremblingly told him "I had grown since he saw me last, and that by the time I was mustered in I would grow some more, and that I would drum and fight, if it should prove actually necessary."

Thus I pleaded with him for fully one hour. Finally he said, "Well, damned if I don't muster you in, just to get rid of you. Sergeant, make out this young devil's papers and let him go and get killed." My heart leaped into my mouth. I tried to thank him, but he would not have it. He hurried me through, and at 5:30 P. M., September 15, 1863, I was a United States soldier. And when I donned that uniform, what a looking soldier! The smallest clothes they issued looked on me as if it would make a suit for my entire family, but in spite of the misfit, I took them and put them on, with the pants legs rolled up to the knees, and the overcoat dragging on the ground.

I went out of that office as proud as a peacock, but a laughing-stock for the boys, and all who gazed at me. I think even the old horse smiled and looked askance; he acted as if I was fooling him, and hungry as he was, when he turned towards the stable, he dragged along as if he either were sorry or ashamed to draw me among people; but I cared not for their jeers and laughs. I was now a soldier and anxious to get home. I pictured the feeling and joyous greetings of my brothers and sister as they would see me ride up in my uniform; how the boys would envy me, and how the sister would throw her arms about me and kiss me, and how her bosom would heave with pride as she gazed upon the uniform that covered her hero brother. Oh! I pictured it all in my boyish fancy, and hastened all my arrangements, so full of joy that I could scarcely eat. I would not wait till morning, but started home about midnight, arriving there just at sunrise.

Chapter 3

First Fire at Fort Powhatan

It was on the 17th of September, 1863, one of those bright, balmy days that we have in good old New England, seated in a "gig," might be seen the writer of this little sketch, dressed in soldiers' clothes, covered by one of those familiar cape overcoats that nearly covered the "gig" and poor old horse. I felt as proud as if I was the general in command of all the army.

Instead of giving the family a surprise, they had heard of my enlisting from the stage-driver, and I found them all in tears. But when I made my appearance tears changed to laughter, for the sight of me I think was enough to give them hope. They didn't believe our government would have such a little, ill-dressed soldier. And father said, after looking me all over: "Well, if they have mustered you in, after they see you in that uniform it will be muster out, my boy."

In about ten days I received orders to report in Augusta. Then the family realized there was more in it than they at first thought, but consoled themselves with the belief that when I reached headquarters, I would be found useless, and sent home. I went away, leaving them with that feeling of hope struggling behind their copious tears. And the lingering kiss of my little step-sister, and her soft sobbing, "Don't, don't, please don't go," as she hung around my neck, ran constantly in my mind from that time till now. All through the nights, on the long marches, in all my troubles, that soft, sweet voice was calling, "George, please, please, don't go." And I could see her little form, and her ever-thoughtful face, a guiding star and a compass that ever guided me away from the shoals and quicksands. She was an angel companion to me all through the trials and hardships of that awful war.

Well, I arrived in Portland, was sent to the barracks with three or four thousand others, was allotted a hard bunk, and then for the first time did I realize what I was doing, what I had committed myself to, and I think if I could have caught that mustering officer I should have appealed to him just as hard to muster me out, as I did to muster me in; but I was in it and must stay. I will never forget the first day of my soldier experience. With what feeling of awe and thumping of my cowardly, timid heart, I heard the different commands of the officers. The disciplining began; the routine of a soldier's life had really started right in Portland, far away from the front where I had only expected to find it. I was detained in those barracks only a few days, and the tap of the drum, and the sound of the bugle as they sounded their different calls, had grown monotonous to me; I no longer regarded them with awe, but with mockery. I wanted to go to the front where the real life of a soldier was known, where glory could be won. I wanted the reality, not boy's play.

I was glad when I was numbered among a squad of about 200 who had orders to go to Washington. That night we marched down to the depot and were crowded into cars. I did not care; I was overjoyed: I was delighted at the prospects of going to the seat of war, near the front, where I thought I might hear the booming of the cannon, and to a place where I would soon be forwarded to my regiment. We arrived in Boston, and to my disappointment, were laid over. We were marched to the barracks on Beach Street, which in early days was the "Beach Street Theatre." The seats, benches, gallery, stage and scenery were all there, and we were crowded into this old, unused temple of Thespis to select a place to sleep where best we could, on the floor, or anywhere. Here I began to grow sick of soldiering; we were in this old musty theatre with a guard over us, not allowed to go on the street, and unable to find out how long we were to be incarcerated there, for we were treated more like prisoners than men who had volunteered to serve their country.

I thought it a great hardship at that time, and kicked at it loud and hard, without any result that benefited us; but since I have been through it all, I can see where it was absolutely necessary to use the rigid and seemingly ungrateful discipline. Well, we were kept in the old theatre for about a week; we were allowed out for two hours each day on passes, and in the evening we sang songs and "acted" on the stage. Each one who could recite or do anything did it, and it was appreciated by a deadhead audience, something unusual nowadays. It was here in this old Beach Street Theatre that my future life was undoubtedly mapped out; from that time I was impressed with a desire to become an actor, and there is no doubt that the seed was planted then and grew and increased in after years.

On the 11th of November, we were ordered to Washington, and embarked on the steamboat train via Fall River, and I shall never forget when we arrived in New York, the demonstration, the greeting, the cheers, the God-speeds that we received as we marched through the city to the ferry, and it seemed to me that I was the one all this was meant for; I thought I was a hero. It seemed that all eyes were on me, and perhaps they were, for among all those Maine giants I belied my state, for I was a dot only, a pigmy beside those mighty woodsmen.

We arrived in Washington without mishap. I was granted permission to go over the city, and then to report to the commanding officer of the camp at Alexandria. My first desire when I found myself with a privilege in the great capital was to visit President Lincoln, have a talk with him and also with Secretary Stanton. My admiration for those two men was almost love, and I fancied, now that I was a soldier, that I could easily meet them; that they would grasp me by the hand, compliment and shower me with congratulations and advice. It is needless to say that I found out that I had overestimated my importance; I did not discuss the war situation with either of those gentlemen. I was a little crestfallen at not meeting them, but contented myself by looking over the city; and wherever I went I noticed I was scrutinized by everybody; soldiers on guard would come to a halt, hesitate and then present arms; some officers would pass me by, then turn and look me over from head to foot; others would touch their caps and then turn and watch me with a kind of wondering gaze, as much as to say, "What is it?"

I forgot to mention that while in Portland I had a tailor make me a very handsome suit of military clothes. He was as ignorant of the regulation style as I was. He only knew the colours and knew that I wanted it nice and handsome. He made it and so covered it over with gold braid and ornaments, that you could not tell whether I was a drum-major or a brigadier-general; that accounted for the salutations and looks of astonishment I received.

The first night I was tired out and started for Alexandria; arrived at headquarters about midnight, and told the sentry I must see the colonel. He thought I had important messages, or was some officer, and escorted me to the colonel's quarters. I woke him up, told him I had reported and wanted a bed.

The colonel said, "Is that all you want? Corporal, put this man in the guard-house." He did!

That was my first experience, and I always after tried to avoid guard-houses. The next morning I was given a broom and put to sweeping around camp with about twenty tough-looking customers. The broom did not look well with my uniform, and as soon as an officer noticed me, I was summoned before the colonel in command. He asked, what I was? I told him I didn't know yet—would not know 'till I reached my regiment. He had a hearty laugh at my appearance; said I ought to be sent to some fair instead of the front. However, he detailed me as his orderly. I held this position some time, until one day there was going to be a squad of recruits, and returned furloughed men sent on a steam-barge to the front at City Point, where Butler was bottled up. I asked to be one of them. The colonel told me I was foolish, and better stay with him, but I insisted; and he allowed me to go. The barge was a kind of an open double-deck boat without cabin or shelter, and they crowded us on to her as thick as we could stand; we were like sardines. I secured a position against the smoke-stack, and before we reached Chesapeake bay I was glad of it, for it became

OUR TROOPS PASSING THROUGH WASHINGTON TO THE FRONT

bitterly cold, and I curled down around this smoke-stack, went to sleep, and when I awoke in the morning I was crisp, dirty, and nearly roasted alive. We crossed the bay in the afternoon. Oh, wasn't it rough! This old river barge would roll and pitch out of sight at times, and we were all wet from head to foot. Then I began to wish myself home on the farm again; but I was in for it, and could not back out. I had one thought that buoyed me up, the thought of meeting my brother.

That evening we passed by Fortress Monroe, up the James River. There was not much transpired to relieve the monotony or appease our hunger or thirst; in fact, it began to look dubious as to reaching City Point. The monotony, however, was somewhat relieved in the morning. About daylight a commotion was caused by the sound of distant cannonading. Every one crowded to the front of the boat; everybody was asking questions of everybody. Each one had some idea to offer as to the cause. Some ventured to say it was a gunboat up the river practising. One old chap, who had evidently been to the front, facetiously claimed that it was the corks out of Butler's bottles. The river was very crooked at this point, and you could not see very far; but presently we rounded a bend in the river, which revealed to us where the cannonading came from, but for what, we could not make out. About a mile ahead of us lay a United States gunboat, and every few minutes a puff of smoke, and then a loud bang—*erang—erang—erang*—with its long vibrations on that still morning, awoke a sense of fear in everyone aboard that boat. No one could account for the situation. Even the captain of the barge stood with pallid cheek, seemingly in doubt what to do as he rang the bell to slow down; but on—on we kept moving—nearer and nearer this most formidable war-ship, and as we did so the shots became more frequent. Then we noticed a man on the bank waving a flag back and forth, up and down in a wild, excited sort of a way. I asked what that meant. An old soldier said the man was signalling the boat to let them know they had hit the target.

Suddenly we were brought to an understanding of what it all meant, for we could now hear the musketry very plain, and could even see the rebels on the banks of the river. At this point a "gig" from the gunboat pulled alongside and gave orders to the captain "to land those troops at once," telling him at the same time that this was Fort Powhatan landing; that Fitzhugh Lee with his cavalry had swooped down upon the garrison, which was only composed of two hundred negro troops, and that they must be re-enforced. The captain protested, as the troops on board were all unarmed, being returned furloughed men and recruits; but it was no use, the order was imperative, and the captain headed his barge toward the shore. There was no wharf. That had been burnt, so he was obliged to run as far as he could onto the sand, then land us overboard. I tell you as that boat neared toward the shore, my face felt as if it were marbleized; sharp twinges ran up and down my whole body, and I'll bet that I was the picture of a coward. I was not the only one. I looked them all over, every one looked just as I felt. One man who stood near me, I know, was more frightened than I, for he was so frightened he smelt badly. But I didn't blame any of those poor men; it was not the pleasantest thing in the world to be placed before the enemy as we were. However, we all landed.

The firing above us on the bank became more intense. An officer who was on the boat with us, returning from a leave of absence, assumed command. He ordered us to fall into line, and marched us into a little ravine, halted, and told us the position and necessity of the occasion. He said the fort was a very important position, and must be held at all hazards; that there were only two hundred coloured troops there, and they could not hold it. Now, he proposed, as we had no arms, to go in with a rush and a yell, and make those rebels think that re-enforcements had arrived. All this time the musketry firing was increasing. The whizz of bullets through the air and about our heads were becoming too frequent. I was in the front rank, centre of the line, and I tell you I think I had a little of that frightened smell about me at this time. Whether it was that or my looks or what, the officer probably took pity on me and told me to skirmish in the rear. I hardly knew where the rear was, but I thought it would be safer under the bank of the river, and there I hastened, and none

BATTLE BETWEEN MONITOR AND MERRIMACK OFF FORTRESS MONROE

too soon, for the rebels had made a break through the lines and poured several volleys into our poor, unarmed re-enforcements. The rebs became more cautious, and that was what was wanted, as the only hope we had was to hold them at bay until re-enforcements could arrive.

Well, I skirmished in the rear, and I found it hotter than the front, for the rebs would crawl to the bank at either end of the breastworks and kept a cross-fire up and down the river. Under and against the banking, there was a sort of old barn; this was filled with hay. The bullets were flying around so thickly that I squeezed myself behind this barn, and after I was well in, the bullets just rained against that old building; but I felt pretty secure till I looked up overhead—I saw that while I was in safety from bullets, a worse danger threatened me. The overhanging bank was liable to cave in and bury me alive.

The uncertainty of my position became more and more apparent. Each moment the increased storm of bullets on the barn prevented me from even looking out, and the constant rattling down of dirt and pebbles from above, told me plainly what a position I was in. I tell you I wished then I had never been mustered in. The uncertainty of my position was soon developed. I came to myself and found I was buried to my neck; my head and face were cut and bleeding, and a soldier was trying to wipe the sand from my eyes and ears. I found I had not been shot, but the banking had caved in and buried me. Gen. "Baldy" Smith, who was in command, happened to see me behind the barn just as the bank caved in. It was he who put the soldiers at work to rescue me. As soon as I was out, and the dust out of my eyes, the general rode down to the beach, leading an extra horse; he called to me. Ordered me to mount. I did so. He made me his orderly.

CHAPTER 4

The 8th Maine

A new danger. I was to carry dispatches across the field, but I did not now have the fear I did at first. I did not mind the sound of the bullets. I became accustomed to it, and I rode back and forth all day long without a scratch. I believe I was so small that I rode between those bullets, and from that time forth I had no fear. I felt as though I were bullet-proof. I felt as if it were ordained that I should go through the war unscathed and unscarred. It did seem so, for I would go through places where it rained bullets, and come out without a scratch. This was my experience all through, and was commented on by comrades, who said I had a charmed life. Well, the day wore away the rebs making feints first at one point, then another. Finally they concentrated their forces against one point, and would have carried it, too, but just then a steamboat loaded with troops rounded the bend of the river. Well, the shouts that went up from the handful of brave soldiers at the sight of that boat I never can forget. The boys on the boat caught the sound. They took in the situation, and answered back the shout with three long, hearty cheers. It created consternation in the rebel lines. They knew the jig was up, but they drew up in line, like dare-devils that they were, and with a cool deliberation, poured volley after volley into the side of the steamer until her nose touched the shore. Well, to see those soldiers leave that steamer was a sight never to be forgotten. They jumped overboard from every part of her. It did not seem five minutes from the time she touched shore until the banks were swarming with our boys in blue. The rebels had taken to flight—

our boys followed some distance, and then returned, relieving us and allowing us to embark again for City Point. After the rebels had retreated, I went outside the breastworks, and the sight that met my eyes on every side would curdle the blood of stouter hearts than mine. It appeared that Lee, with his cavalry, had surprised the pickets, and being negroes, every one they captured they would hang up to a tree after they were mutilated. I saw several with fingers cut off in order to obtain a ring quickly, and many other sickening sights which tended to make me a hardened soldier. I was having lots of experience, even before I had really reached my regiment, and I tell you, the heroic ardour of my boyish dream was beginning to ooze out of me quite fast. I began to think I was not cut for a soldier.

Well, my first battle was over, my first experience before an enemy. The first sound of musketry had died away, and we were again steaming towards City Point to join our regiments. We arrived there the next night about ten o'clock. There didn't seem to be any one in command of us or any one to direct us. It was very dark on shore, but in the distance you could see a glaring light above the horizon, as if there was a long building on fire. But from the occasional sound of guns from that quarter, I made up my mind it was the advance line of our army.

It was Butler's command, and our regiment, the Eighth Maine, must be there. The Eighth Maine, Company H, was the regiment and company to which my brother belonged, and in which I was enlisted. I started out across the fields in the direction of the light—on, on I tramped, into ditches, through mires, over fences.

The farther I went the faster I went. I was so impatient I could not hold myself to a walk; it was a dog-trot all the time. I was heedless of every obstacle, till I began to near the front. I realized the danger by the whizzing of shell, and the zip, zip of bullets. I found myself among lots of soldiers, and how ragged and dirty the poor fellows looked.

I asked the first man I came to where the Eighth Maine was? He looked at me in perfect astonishment. "This is the Eighth, what's left of it." I asked him if he knew where my brother was—Charley Ulmer? "Oh, yes," he said, and pointing to a little group of men, who were round a wee bit of a fire; "there he is, don't you know him?"

I hesitated, for really I could hardly tell one from the other. He saw my bewilderment, and took me by the arm and led me over to the fire. They all started and stared at me, and to save my life I could not tell which was my brother; but one more ragged than the rest uttered a suppressed cry, rushed forward, and throwing his arm about my neck, sobbed and cried like a child. "My God! my brother! Oh George, George, why did you come here?" His grief seemed to touch them all, for they all began to wipe their eyes with their ragged coat-sleeves. This began to tell on me, and for the next ten minutes it was a kind of a blubbering camp. After awhile they reconciled themselves, and began to ply me with questions faster than I could answer. My brother sat down with me and lectured me very soundly for coming, as there was no need of it. He gave a graphic description of the hardships they had endured, and I can never obliterate the picture he presented that night. His clothes were ragged and patched, begrimed with smoke, grease and dirt; his hat an old soft one, with part of the rim gone and the crown perforated with bullet holes; his beard scraggly and dirty; his big toes peeping out of a pair of old boots with the heels all run down, in fact, he was a sight—a strong contrast to my tailor-made suit. I will never forget the expression on my brother's face when about half an hour after my arrival he looked up to me with his eyes half full of tears glistening on that dirty face, and with a kind of cynical smile, asked, after looking me over and over: "What are you, anyhow?"

I told him I didn't know.

"Well, after you have been here awhile, those pretty clothes won't look as they do now, and you will probably find out what you are after you have dodged a few shells."

Our conversation was brought to a climax by orders to break camp and fall in. We learned we were going to embark somewhere on a boat; everything was hustle-bustle now; little sheltered tents were struck, tin cups, canteens, knapsacks were made ready, and in about fifteen minutes that begrimed, dirty, hungry family of Uncle Sam's was on the march to the river. We were marched on board an old ferry-boat, and crowded so thickly that we could scarcely stand. My brother seemed now to feel that he had the responsibility of my comfort, even my life, on his hands—and being a favourite he elbowed me a place at the end of the boat, where we could sit down by letting our feet hang over the end of the boat. In that position we remained. We didn't have room to stand up and turn around. I was awful sleepy, but dared not go to sleep for fear I would fall overboard. Finally my brother fixed me so I could lay my head back, and he held on to me while I slept.

CHAPTER 5

Cold Harbor

The next morning we landed at a place called West Point, on the York river; why we landed there we didn't know. Of course soldiers never did know anything of the whys and wherefores; they only obeyed orders, stood up or laid down and got killed—they had no choice in the matter. Well, we landed, and I tell you, we were stiff and hungry. While they were unloading the horses, which was done by lowering them into the water and letting them swim ashore, which took some time, they allowed us a chance to skirmish for food. About half a mile from the river were a dozen houses—nice-looking places. Towards these we started; they were all closed up; they all looked deserted; there was not a sign of life, except the cackle of hens or chickens in the hen-house. Chickens were good enough for us, and I was one of the first to get to the pen; secured two handfuls of chicks, and was just emerging with them when a big woman confronted me; she stood and looked me straight in the eye, and with both hands held on to a mastiff, that to me looked as big as an ox.

"How dare you?" said she.

"I don't," said I.

"What are you doing with my chickens, you good-for-nothing Yankee thief?"

I tried to apologize, but it was no use. Even my pretty uniform had no more effect than my eloquence. I simply put Mr. and Mrs. Chicks down and backed out of the yard. She was good enough to hold on to the dog, for which I was very grateful. I think I had more respect for the dog than the lady.

44

However, I had to resort to pork and hard tack for my breakfast. About noon that day we began our march. Where we were going, everybody guessed, but none knew. I didn't care. I was now a kind of a half-settled soldier, but from the first, I was a kind of privileged character. No one gave me orders. No one seemed to claim me. I had never been assigned to any company. I never had to answer roll-call. I could go and come as I pleased. Once in awhile a guard would halt me, but not often. They didn't know what I was, and they didn't care. All the afternoon we marched. Our route was along the railroad, the rails of which had the appearance of being recently torn up by the rebels. About four o'clock I was becoming very tired. We came to a clearing, and some distance in the field was a darky ploughing with a mule. I made a break for him, and the rest of that march I rode. No one objected, but the boys shouted as I made my appearance on the mule; a mile or two further along we sighted a farm-house. I drew reins on my mule and made for the house; I made the boys glad on my return, for I secured a demijohn of applejack, a big bundle of tobacco, and a box of eggs. That successful raid gave me courage, and I began to think that was what I was destined for, and I liked it first-rate, for it was a pleasure to me to see those poor, hungry boys have any delicacy, or even enough of ordinary food.

That night we had to halt, for the rebs had burned the bridge, and we had to wait for pontoons. The boys were tired and hungry. A guard was posted to prevent any foraging, but I was a privileged character, and I bolted through the lines. I had seen some pigs and calves scamper into the swamp about half a mile back from where we halted, and thinking a bit of fresh meat would be nice for the boys, I determined to have some. Cautiously I stole away, till I arrived at the edge of the swamp; and such a jungle! It was almost impossible to penetrate it, so I skirted the edge, hoping to see a pig emerge. After tramping an hour I was rewarded by seeing a calf. I drew my revolver, sneaked up and fired at poor bossy. It dropped—I was a good shot—but when I reached the poor beast I found it was as poor as a rail and covered with sores as big as my hand. I was disappointed, but cut off as much as I could that was not sore, and took it to camp. We put the kettles on the fires in short order, and my brother's company had fresh meat broth—the first fresh meat in a month—and I tell you it was good, even if it had been sore. After that episode Company H claimed me and dubbed me their mascot. I accepted the position, and from that time forth I devoted my time to foraging, stealing anything I could for my company, and I doubt if there was a company in the whole army that fared better than ours, for I was always successful in my expeditions.

After a long, tedious march across pontoons, over corduroy roads, we confronted the Johnnies at Cold Harbor. It was here that I found myself in a real, genuine battle. I got lost in the scuffle. I found myself amidst bursting shell and under heavy musketry fire. I was bewildered and frightened. I did not know which way to go. I ran this way and that, trying to find my brother and regiment. Every turn I made it seemed I encountered more bullets and shells. Soldiers were shouting and running in every direction, artillery was galloping here and there, on every side it seemed they were fighting for dear life. On one side of me I saw horses and men fall and pile up on top of each other. Cannon and caissons with broken wheels were turned upside down, riderless horses were scampering here and there, officers were riding and running in all directions, the shells were whizzing through the air, and soldiers shouting at the top of their voices. Everything seemed upside down. I thought the world had come to an end. I tried to find shelter behind a tree, away from the bullets, but as soon as I found shelter on one side it seemed as though the bullets and shells came from all sides, and I lay down in utter despair and fright. I don't know how long I was there, but when I awoke I thought the war was over, it was so still. I thought every one had been killed on both sides, excepting myself. I was just thinking I would try and find a live horse, ride back to Washington and tell them that the war was over, everybody was killed, when my brother tapped me on the shoulder and asked me where I had been. He had gone through it all, escaped with the loss of one toe, and had come to the rear to have it dressed and find me.

Desperate Charge of Confederates to Capture a Union Battery

The next morning I was sent with the "Stretcher Corps" under a flag of truce to the battle field to help take the wounded to the rear and bury the dead, and when we reached the scene, how well could I imagine what the awful struggle had been. The worst of the great conflict had occurred in an orchard, and there the sight was most appalling; dead and dying heroes were lying about as thick as a slumbering camp would be, sleeping with their guns for pillows the night before a battle; to many of those poor fellows it was that sleep that knows no waking, while to others it was the awaking from unconsciousness by the twinges of a mortal gaping wound, awake just long enough to get a glimpse of the Gates Ajar, sink back and start on that journey from which no traveller returns.

Blue and the gray were mingled together on this awful field of slaughter, and both sides seemed to respect the solemnity by a cessation of hostilities, and the hushed silence was only broken by the painful cry of some helpless wounded, or dying groans of others. The little white cloth we wore around our arms to denote, we belonged to the stretcher corps, seemed to add to the sadness of the occasion, for to those poor wounded souls we were like ministering angels, and as I moved from one to the other with tear dimmed eyes offering water and assistance to those who needed it I saw many incidents of bravery and self-sacrifice that went far toward ameliorating the suffering and obliterating the bitterness of the blue and the gray. I noticed one poor fellow who had spread his rubber blanket to catch the dew of the night sharing the moisture thus gathered with an unfortunate confederate who had lost a leg. Another, a confederate was staying the life-blood of a union officer by winding his suspenders around the mangled limb. Oh! the horror of such a picture can never be penned—or told, and contemplated only by soldiers who have been there.

One-half of our regiment had been killed or wounded. After this things settled down into a siege. I employed my time foraging for the company. One day I found an apple orchard, gathered as many apples as I could carry, took them to the company and made apple-sauce without sweetening. They ate very heartily of it, poor fellows. It was a treat for them; but it was a bad find, for the next day the whole lot of them were unfit for duty. That nearly put a stop to my reconnoitring. Our regiment lay here in the advance line of breastworks for thirteen days. The sappers and miners were constantly working our breastworks towards the enemy, and every time I wanted to reach my company I found it in a new place and more difficult to reach. The rebel sharpshooters, with their deadly aim, were waiting for such chaps as me. However, under cover of night, I always managed to find and reach the company with some palatable relish.

I will never forget one night; four men were detailed to go to the rear for rations. The commissary was located about two miles to the rear, and the wagon could only haul the rations within one mile of us on account of jungle and rebel sharpshooters. Therefore these men were detailed to pack the rations the rest of the way. I was one of the detail from my company. We went back to the covered wagons that were waiting for us. The boys said I was too small to walk, and they threw me into the rear end of one of the wagons. We got to the commissary tent—a long tent open at both ends—and from both ends they weighed out the rations of coffee, sugar, etc. While the soldier who was doing the weighing on one end had his back turned, I managed to fill my haversack from a full barrel of coffee that stood at the end of the tent. I had two haversacks for that purpose, for I went there with that intent; but I came away with only one filled. I could not get a chance for the other; it was on the wrong side. Finally the rations were all aboard, and we started back. The boys repeated the operation of throwing me into the wagon again, and there was my opportunity. I would fill my other haversack from the bags in the wagon; that's what the boys expected I would do, and I did from the first bag I could get into. Each company had its own bag.

Petersburg

When we arrived at the breastworks my company crowded around me for plunder. I divided it up, and was looked upon as quite a hero, but when the rations were issued it was found our company's bag was short about thirty rations of sugar, but no one said a word. It was surmised that it got spilled. Day after day our regiment lay there and our army did not seem to gain anything. I was becoming disgusted and discouraged.

One night the Johnnies made a charge on us. That was the only time I ever fired a gun in the whole war, and I honestly believe I killed a dozen men, for immediately after they stopped firing. It was only a few moments, however; on they came, only to be repulsed. They kept that up nearly all night, and I served my country by standing down in the trench, loading a gun and passing it up to my brother to fire. I did this all night, but I didn't see any less rebels in the morning. Our next order was to fall back, under cover of darkness.

We fell back about a mile and halted for some reason, I thought to get breakfast. Anyway I built a little fire behind a stone wall, put my coffee-pot on and the remnants of a pot of beans. They were getting nice and hot; my brother and I stood waiting, smacking our lips in the anticipation of a feast, when whizz came one of those nasty little "Cohorn" mortar shells and it dropped right into our coffee and beans.

Then the bugle sounded, "fall in," and we started with downcast hearts and empty stomachs, and a longing good-bye to the debris of beans and coffee. It was a tiresome march. Of course, we didn't know where we were going, and that made it all the longer.

We eventually brought up at White-House landing on the York river, where we were put on board of a steam transport without being given time to draw rations. From there we steamed down the York and up the James river to the Appomattox, and up the river to Point of Rocks. We landed here on the Bermuda Hundred side, in the rear of Butler's works, obtained some bread and coffee, and then crossed the Appomattox on pontoons and pushed on towards Petersburg. Our regiment belonged at that time to the 2nd brigade, 2nd division of the 18th corps, commanded by Major General "Baldy" Smith.

We soon met the enemy's pickets in front of Petersburg. They fled before that long, serpentine file of blue-coats like deer. On, on we went. We could see the rebels running in their shirt sleeves, throwing coats, guns and everything in their mad flight. I don't think there was a shot fired on either side 'till we reached a fort, Smith I think it was called. It was just at dusk. This fort was located on a mound or hill with a ravine in front of it. Our brigade was drawn up in line of battle in a wheat-field on the right. A coloured brigade was ordered to charge the fort from the hill opposite, and across this ravine; then I beheld one of the grandest and most awful sights I ever saw; those coloured troops started on a double quick, and as they descended the hill, the fort poured volley after volley into them. The men seemed to fall like blades of grass before a machine, but it did not stop them; they rallied and moved on; it was only the work of a few minutes. With a yell they were up and into that fort, and in less time than it takes to tell it, the guns were turned on the fleeing rebels. Here was the greatest mistake of our greatest commander. All of our army was brought to a standstill by some one's foolish order. Not another move was made. We lay there waiting, and all night long we could hear the trains rumbling along on the other side of the Appomattox river. Lee had been outwitted. We had stolen a march on him. We had arrived in front of defenceless Petersburg, and could have gone right in and on to Richmond without a struggle. But that fatal order to halt gave him all night

My First Day in Front of Petersburg

to hurry his forces from Cold Harbor, and in the morning we found plenty of determined rebels in front of us, and thereby the war was prolonged months and hundreds and thousands of lives lost. I swore all night. I kicked and condemned every general there was in the army for the blunder I saw they were making. I only wished I could be the general commanding for one hour. But it was no use; I couldn't be.

I was nothing but a boy. But I had my ideas. I thought, perhaps, more than some of the officers did. I kept myself posted on facts and the topography of the country. The dispositions of generals was a matter of grave importance to me. I believed generals should be selected to command, *not* for their qualifications in military tactics alone, *not* because they had graduated well-dressed from "West Point," but for their indomitable pluck, judgment and honesty of purpose. It did seem to me that some of our best officers were invariably placed in the most unimportant positions and commands. Take, for instance, "Custer's" Brigade of daring men, headed by those intrepid officers, Alger and Towns, wasting their time and imperilling the lives of thousands of good soldiers around Emettsburg, Gordonsville, Bottom Bridge, carrying out the foolish orders of superiors in command. Why could not these officers of cool judgment be with us at this critical moment?—they made *their* victories, what would they have done had they the great opportunities that were presented to others who failed?

All night about the camp-fire the boys would delight in nagging me—getting me into arguments and debates. They called me the "midget orator of the Army of the Potomac." I will never forget one night soon after the advance on Petersburg; we were clustered about with coffee cups and pipes; an argument waxed warm in regard to the possibilities of the war lasting two more years; finally I was called upon for my views. "Midget," said Col. McArthur, "if you had supreme command of our army, what would you do?"

What would I do? If Uncle Sam would give me one regiment from each State in the Union—give me Grant, Burnside, Sherman, Sheridan, Custer, Alger, Hooker, Hancock, Thomas and Siegel to command them, I would take Richmond and settle the rebellion before they had time to wire and ask Stanton if I should. This was received with cheering and applause. But my boyish fancies and ideas were never gratified; I never had the pleasure of seeing my ideal army together, and Richmond was not taken for many months afterward.

The Forager

A few days after our regiment was drawn up in line of battle in a wheat field. It was just nightfall. I was lying down on the bank of a ditch waiting for the move-forward. Suddenly a shell came over my head and bust right in the centre of my company. I thought I saw legs and arms flying in all directions.

I started on the dead run for the rear. I believed I was going right, but it seemed as if the shells were coming from our own guns in the rear. I thought they had mistaken us for the enemy. I could see the shells coming, and every time they would fire, I would fall on my stomach, and thought they all went just over my head. I was soon, however, out of range, and began to feel easy, when a new fear took possession of me. What if I had, in my bewilderment, run into the rebel lines? I saw just ahead of me an old-fashioned southern mansion, with a high board fence all around it, and in the enclosure several small cabins used for the slaves to live in. I could not remember seeing this before, so I made up my mind I was actually inside rebeldom. However, I decided to make the best of it, and if I were or were not I would see if I could find something to eat. With fear and faltering steps I moved toward the big gate, swung it open, and it gave an awful squeak as it swung on its old rusty hinges. There was not a sign of life in or about the place, and that gave me hope and courage. In the centre of the yard was a large hen-house. Cautiously toward this I crawled, heard the cackle of fowl, went first on one side then on the other, looking for the door; and imagine my surprise, the fear that took possession of me—my hair stood on end; for sitting there on a bench back of this hen-house were two big Johnnies. I couldn't speak, I couldn't move, till one of them said, "Good evening, sar; got anything to eat?"

"Yes, yes," I stammered, "I have some hard-tack."

Finally, one of them seeing I was most scared to death, spoke up and said, "Don't be alarmed; we are only deserters and want to give ourselves up; show us to headquarters."

I was brave now. I gave them what hard-tack I had, and marched them ahead of me back to the rear, till we found headquarters. Afterward, I was offered a furlough for capturing two of the enemy. I never told this before; I took the credit. But I was not satisfied; I'd rather have some of those chickens than live rebels. So back I went and I got five; started back to the rear, put a kettle on a fire and boiled them, kept them three days, till I found my brother and the remnant of the regiment. When I did find them I made their hearts glad by showing them the boiled chickens. They were awful hungry and set to eating with a ravenous appetite, but they could not eat them, hungry as they were. I had no salt, and so put a big chunk of salt beef in the pot instead of salt, consequently the chickens were saltier then Lot's wife.

I think I felt more disappointed than anybody, so I determined to make up for it in some other way. The regiment finally brought up in the first or advance line of breastwork, and I was still skirmishing in the rear for anything that I could find that was good.

I had tramped back to the rear about three miles, my mind bent on securing anything that would please the heart and eye, or tickle the palates of the brave fellows who had gone to face the enemy and do the real work of our country. About a quarter of a mile to the left of me I espied a covered wagon moving toward the front. I wondered what it was and where it was bound for, as from the frequent halt it made, it seemed the driver was lost to himself. I bore down toward him and found it was a sanitary wagon, loaded with good things sent out by the ladies of the north. The driver was an old man—one of those long, lanky individuals who might be taken for a parson or a horse dealer.

He reminded me of the "Arkansaw Traveller." His clothes were of the salt and pepper homespun goods, a little worse for wear and very ill fitting, they looked as if he had lost fifty pounds of flesh since he started from home; his pants were tucked into a pair of old cow-hide boots; his hat was a cross between a stove pipe and a derby; his hair was red, very long and sprinkled with grey; his eyebrows were shaggy, nearly meeting over the nose and hanging down over a pair of faded blue eyes. So wrinkled was his skin that you would think his face was a frozen laugh; a little strip of red hair ran down the side of his face in front of his ears and almost met under his chin; the space left open in his whiskers, evidently an outlet for the tobacco juice that trickled down from each side of his mouth. As I approached he pulled up his mules and called to me in a rather cracked voice, "Say, Major, or Sergeant, or what ever you are, whar's the field hospital?"

"Three miles from here," said I, pointing backward.

"What's that firin' I hear? Ain't no rebs 'round yere, be thar?"

"Yes," I replied; "there's a long row of them about half a mile in front of us, and you had better halt right where you are. What's your cargo?"

"Wall, I got most anything that is needed by you poor fellows—useful things. I'm sent here by a society called the North-field First Methodist Ladies' Relief and Sanitary Association. They selected me for my courage to go to the front and distribute this load. But I guess I'll have to go too near that row of rebs if I'd give them out in person. I'll unhitch here and feed my mules. You don't think thar's any danger of them grey-coats disturbing me, do you? I should hate to have all these good things fall into their hands."

I inquired what he had, to which he replied with apparent amazement: "Shirts, stockin's, bakin' powder, condensed milk, canned apples, peaches, Boston beans, tobacco, hair oil, tooth powder, cathartic pills, Jamaiki ginger, and fine tooth combs— Whoa thar—stop your infernal kickin'. Them durned mules are worse than two-year-old heifers."

The wearied animals had become all tangled up in the harness, and I thought I'd steal some of the eatables for my company while he was freeing and feeding the mules. He gave me a better opportunity however. There was a patch of peanuts or groundnuts a short distance away. He asked me to mind his mules while he went to see what they were and how they grew. When he left me I got into the wagon and loaded myself down with everything until I could carry no more. Then I conceived an idea, and if he would only remain away long enough I could carry the thing out. I found a small hatchet in the wagon, and with my tin cup began digging a hole near the wagon. I worked like a beaver for awhile, at the same time keeping my eye on the peanut patch. The size of the receptacle would be determined by the length of time the old man remained away. Finally I got a hole made about the size of a bushel basket, and thought I'd take no more chances. I scrambled into the wagon and threw out cans of milk, etc., until the hole was completely filled. I had just nicely covered it up when my friend returned and asked:

"What *you* been diggin' for thar—them durned things too? Why, durn them, I'd just as lieve eat raw beans."

I looked up in a guilty sort of way and told him, "I was digging for a shell that lit there while he was gone."

"Gee-whiz! I guess I'd better get out of this place as quick as I can. I say, Mister, whar's your Comp'ny?"

"What's alive of them are at the front, suffering from want and hunger," I replied in a strong manner, thinking perhaps he would drive nearer and distribute his load. But he was bent on going back. As he climbed to his seat he said, "I'll tell you, Mr. Sergeant, you kin take a few of these things to the men that are sick in your company."

"They are all sick," I said quickly, for I was greedy and wanted all I could get. He pulled out a hospital shirt and tied up the neck. Having filled it with condensed milk, tobacco, and other things, he asked me if I could carry it. "Could I! I could carry all there's in your cart," I replied. I found my load was a little heavier than I had expected it to be, but I wouldn't say there was too much, but helped him to hitch up his mules and he started off, after giving me a warm hand-shake. I watched him until he disappeared from view, and then thought I would open up the

The Great Mine Explosion in Front of Petersburg

treasure I had buried and deposit some of the shirtful which he had so kindly given me after I had robbed him. It would lighten the load and I could return for the balance next day. I had just started to dig, when I looked up and saw him driving back as hard as he could drive, "Say, young fellow, I—I—I," in a wild, excited manner, reigning his mules up with a jerk and a "Whoa, thar," loud enough to be heard in Petersburg, "I—I thought I'd drive back and dig up that darned shell. It'll be a great curiosity. When I get home I can show the folks the dangerous position I was placed in while distributing these things."

I didn't stop to hear any more, but hurried away with my shirtful. I ran hard and fast, and didn't dare to turn and look round. The shells began to whiz pretty thickly just at this time, and I prayed and hoped that the old man would get scared and not dig for that shell, for I wanted the boys to have it.

This was on the day fixed for the great mine explosion, every soldier on the entire line was waiting with bated breath for the signal or prolonged rumble of that expected explosion. It did not come, however. The suspense was broken by the appearance nearly a half a mile away, of a soldier with something white on his back, that made a good target for the rebel sharpshooters. Down the railroad I came. I reached the first line of earthworks. For a short distance I would keep on top. In this way I kept on, on, first running one breastwork then another, till I reached the front line. On top of this I ran the whole length, heedless and unmindful of the rebel bullets that pelted about me. I almost flew along. The soldiers shouted to me to keep down, but I heeded them not. Finally I reached the place where my regiment was, jumped down as coolly as if I had run no risk, deposited my bag, received the congratulations of my company, who examined me all over to see if there were any wounds. They found none, however, but on opening the shirt every can of milk had a bullet hole through it, and condensed milk, extract of beef, and tobacco had to be eaten as a soufflé.

Hospital Duty

The next day found me at the rear again. I looked for the buried treasure—found it. Evidently the old gent had been frightened away, for about half the dirt had been removed from the top, and the stuff was not uncovered. There was a desperate fight going on at the right of our line. I was pressed into the service of the stretcher corps, which is usually composed of drummer boys. I did duty at this all the forenoon. The onslaught was terrible, and many poor fellows did I help carry off that field; some to live for an hour, others to lose a limb that would prove their valour and courage for the balance of their lives.

This day our regiment was relieved from the front and supposing they were going to City Point to recruit, they came back about a half a mile, halted for orders; I heard of it and concluded I would go with them and so hastened to where they were, and soon after my arrival the order came to "fall in." They did so with alacrity and bright hopes of much needed rest. I took my drum and place at the head of the regiment and started with them.

The road to the left led to City Point. Imagine their surprise when nearing it, the order came, *"File right, by company into line, double quick march."*

The entire regiment seemed paralyzed for a moment, but only for a moment, the whizzing of the shells and the zip zip of the rebel bullets plainly told them what caused the sudden change. I was dumbfounded, I didn't know what to do. My brother yelled to me to go to the rear quick, but I didn't; I kept on with them until it seemed to rain bullets, but on, on they went unmindful of the awful storm of leaden messengers of death—on, on and into one of the fiercest charges of the entire war. I saw men fall so thick and fast that there didn't seem as if there was any of my regiment left, and I made up my mind it was too hot for me, so started on the dead run to the rear for a place of safety, and I didn't stop until I was pretty sure I was out of harm's way.

I came to a place about one mile back where evidently there had been a battery located; here I sat down to rest and meditate. I examined myself all over to see if I was hit, found I was unhurt but my drum had received several bullet holes in it.

Finding a green spot I stretched myself out and listened to the awful sound of musketry firing which was going on at the front, around me on all sides was the debris of a deserted camp, empty tin cans, broken bayonets, pieces of guns, fragments of bursted shell, and occasionally a whole one that had failed to explode. I had only sat here a few moments thinking which was the best way to go when I was joined by another Drummer Boy from a Pennsylvania regiment. We sat down and talked over our exploits, and I thought he was the most profane lad I had ever met. Most every other word he uttered was an oath.

I asked him if he wasn't afraid to talk so.

"What the h—l should I be afraid of?" he asked, at the same time picking up an old tent stake and sticking it into the ground, trying to drive it in with the heel of his boot. Failing in this

he reached over and got hold of an unexploded shell and used this on the stake, but it was heavy and unwieldy.

"I wonder if this was fired by those d—d rebs," he asked.

"I guess it was," I replied, "and you better look out, or it might go off."

"Off be d—d, their shells were never worth the powder to blow 'em to h—l, see the hole in the butt of it, it would make a G—d—d good mawl, wouldn't it?" and looking round at the same time he found an old broom. Stripping the brush and wire from the handle he said, "I'll make a mawl of it and drive that d—d rebel stake into the ground with one of their own d—d shells, be d—d if I don't." Inserting the broom handle into the end of the shell he walked over to a stump, and taking the shell in both hands commenced pounding onto the stick against the stump; "d—d tight fit," he hollered to me, and the next instant I was knocked down by a terrific explosion. I came to my senses in a minute and hastened to where he had been standing. There the poor fellow lay unconscious and completely covered with blood, there was hardly a shred of clothes on him, his hair was all burned and both hands taken completely off, as if done by a surgeon's saw.

I was excited and horror stricken for a moment. The sight was horrible, but I quickly regained my composure, knowing that something must be done, and done quickly. So taking the snares from my drum I wound them tightly around his wrists to stop the flow of blood, then I hailed an ambulance, and we took him to the held hospital about a mile to the rear.

On the way the poor fellow regained consciousness, and looking at his mutilated wrists, and then with a quick and be-wildered glance at me, "G—d—d tough, ain't it," then the tears started in his eyes, and he broke down and sobbed the rest of the way, "Oh, my God! What will my poor mother say? Oh, what will she do!"

We reached the field hospital, which is only a temporary place for the wounded where the wounds are hurriedly dressed, and then they are sent to regular hospitals, located in Baltimore, Philadelphia, Norfolk, Portsmouth, etc., where they have all the comforts possible. We laid the little fellow down in one corner of the tent to wait his turn with the surgeon, and when I left him, he cried and begged for me to stay, but I couldn't stand his suffering longer, so I bade him good-bye with tears streaming down my own cheeks. I hurried out, and even after I reached the outside I could hear him cry, "Oh, my God! What will my poor mother say? Oh, what will she do!"

In the afternoon I was detailed to wait on the amputating tables at the field hospital.

It was a horrible task at first. My duty was to hold the sponge or "cone" of ether to the face of the soldier who was to be operated on, and to stand there and see the surgeons cut and saw legs and arms as if they were cutting up swine or sheep, was an ordeal I never wish to go through again. At intervals, when the pile became large, I was obliged to take a load of legs or arms and place them in a trench near by for burial. I could only stand this one day, and after that I shirked all guard duty. The monotony, the routine of life, in front of Petersburg, was becoming distasteful to me. I had stolen everything I could. My district or territory had given out, so the next day I started for the front to bid my brother good-bye.

The Pie & Watch

Our regiment was sometimes relieved and ordered to the rear for rest; so it was on this occasion, they had fallen back and halted in a little ravine. I met my brother, who always expected me to bring him some stolen sweets or goodies of some kind, but unfortunately this time I came empty-handed. I had failed to find anything to steal. I was hungry myself, but when I looked at him I forgot my own hunger, for such a forlorn appearance as he presented almost broke my heart, and I determined to find him something to eat at all hazards. So off I started on an independent foraging expedition. I had only gone a short distance when I espied a "pie wagon." Usually when the paymaster was around there would be "hucksters" or peddlers with all kinds of commodities following in his wake.

This fellow had driven to the front from City Point. They were generally dare-devils, and this one was no exception to the rule. He had driven right up to the front, unhitched his horse and began selling hot mince pies. He had some kind of a stove and outfit in an old covered wagon where he made the pies quickly and sold them hot for one dollar apiece; the pies were about the size of a saucer. When I reached the wagon there was quite a crowd around him; some were buying and eating them as if they were good, while others stood looking on wistfully watching their comrades who were fortunate enough to have the price. I was one of the unfortunates. I could smell the cooking of the pies long before I reached the wagon, and this only served to increase my already ravenous hunger; but all I could

do was to stand there with my hands in my pockets, smack my lips and imagine what they tasted like—the longer I stayed the better they tasted. I believe I would have given five hundred dollars for one if I had possessed the money, but I didn't have a cent; our regiment had not been paid. All this time I was thinking of my poor brother, how he would like one of those hot pies, and I began to concoct schemes how to get one. The way I worked the old sanitary man would never do to try on this fellow, for he was a "fakir" by birth, occupation and inclination. The fellow was doing a lively business.

"Here you are! Nice hot pies, fresh baked, right from the oven! Walk up lively here. Only one dollar apiece! There's only a few of them left, and I shan't be here again for a month; walk up with your dollar! Get off that wheel, you young devil!"

I had climbed up on the wheel to make observations and see if I couldn't sneak a pie, but he was watching and detected my motive; so down I got and stood gaping at him, my mouth wide open; but my hungry look had no effect on him, he had no sympathy for anything except dollars. Finally I thought my brother might have a dollar, so back to him I ran, told him of the pies, but he had not a cent. The knowledge of the pies added two fold to his hunger. "Gosh!" he said, "ain't there some way? Can't you steal one?" "No," I said, "I have tried that. I would have made his horse run away and upset his wagon, but the darned cuss had unhitched him."

"Gee!" I exclaimed, "I have it." And off I started. Charley, my brother, owned an old-fashioned silver watch, one of those old "English levers." He thought a great deal of it as a keep-sake and always gave it to me to keep when he was going into action. I had this watch now, and made up my mind I would trade it to the "fakir" and get a lot of pies for us all. Oh! such bright anticipations of hot mince pies. I could almost see them floating in the air as big as cart wheels, and fearing they would all be sold before I could reach the wagon, I ran as hard as I could. The crowd had thinned out and so had the pies.

"How many have you got left?" I eagerly asked.

"Oh, plenty," he replied; "how many, do you want?"

"Well," I said, nearly out of breath, "I haven't any money, but I want all you have, and I'll trade you a nice watch for them."

"Say, cully! what yer givin' me? I don't want no watch. Let's see it."

I quickly passed it up to him, and stood working my fingers and feet impatiently and revolving in my mind how many pies he would give me and how I would manage to carry them back, when he broke out into a loud, contemptuous laugh, and passed the watch back.

"Say, young fellow, that ain't no good. I'd rather have a black-ing box than that thing."

"It's silver," I replied.

"That don't make no difference. I'll give you one pie for the thing if you want it, see!"

I turned the watch over and over in my hand, my feelings hurt and my stomach disappointed. Then I thought of my brother, forgot that it was his high-priced time-piece, and quickly said:

"Give me the pie and take the watch."

He did so, and away I started on the dead run, I could hardly resist the temptation of biting the pie; but just before I reached the regiment, and in full sight of my brother, I stumbled and fell, smashing the pie into the dirt and mud. I picked myself up, looked at the crushed pie, and the tears started in my eyes; but only for a moment. I brushed them away, gathered up the pieces and hurried to my brother. We rubbed the mud from the pieces the best we could, and devoured them with a hearty relish. Af-ter the pie was gone, I regretted the bargain that I had made. Pie and watch both gone. Remorse took possession of me. I felt guilty; I was conscience-stricken. I was unsatisfied; no more time, no more pie.

"Gosh, that pie was good, wasn't it, 'Pod'?" This was a nick-name my brother was pleased to call me by.

"Jinks, I wish you had brought more. Why didn't you try and get two?"

"Well," I said, faltering, "you—you see, I—I didn't have time enough."

"Well, how did you get it, anyway?"

72

"Oh! I got it on tick." And then I walked over to a stump, thinking I would get away from his questions and all the time revolving in my mind whether I should tell him the truth, or say I had lost it. I felt ashamed of myself and thought what a darned fool I was. I concluded I wasn't a bit smart—the idea of giving a watch for a pie! Finally, Charley came over to me.

"What time is it, Pod?"

"I—I don't know!"

"Why, ain't the watch going?"

"Yes-s. No, it's gone."

"Gone! What do you mean?" And then divining the truth, he exclaimed: "Gorram it, did you sell the watch for that pie?"

"Yes, Charley, I did, but I couldn't help it; I knew you wanted the pie so bad."

"Gor-rammed little fool; didn't you know better than that?"

Then I saw the great big tears come into his eyes, and I couldn't stand it. I patted him on the back and said: "Never mind, Charley. I'll go and get the watch back if I have to kill the pie man."

So off I started on the dead run, caught the fellow just as he was ready to go. I asked him if I could ride to the rear with him. He answered, "Yes, and you can show me how to get into that turnip watch." So I climbed on to the seat beside him and we started.

I took the watch apart, showed him how it was wound, set and regulated it, and was about to hand it back to him, when a shell burst a short way from us, which frightened his horse so that he cramped the wagon and upset it, and in the confusion I got lost with the watch. On the next day I gave it to my brother and told him how I had obtained it. He laughed at me, and said he "guess I'd better keep it myself," and so put it in his pocket. That night the regiment went into action, and my brother was slightly wounded several times. One shot would have proved fatal, but the watch received the bullet and the wound proved fatal only to the watch; it was smashed all to pieces. But my brother prizes the pieces now more than he ever did the whole watch.

The Veteran Reserve Corps

The next day my regiment was ordered to the front again. I made up my mind I would not go with them. I concluded I needed rest in order to recuperate, so when the regiment started I bade my brother good-bye, gave him a parting kiss and God's blessings, so off I started.

About a half a mile from my regiment I came to one of those Virginia fences, got up on top of it, and sat thinking, and while sitting there the shells began to fly pretty thick. I thought I had better be moving, jumped down, and as I did so a shell struck one of the rails of the fence. A piece of the rail struck me and was harder than I was, for when I came to my senses I found I was in the hospital. I didn't think I was hurt very badly, but when I tried to get up, found I couldn't. From there they moved me to "Balfour Hospital" at Portsmouth, Virginia. I never will forget the shame and mortification I felt at the sight I must have presented when the boat that conveyed us to Portsmouth arrived.

An old negro came to my bunk and took me on his back, and with a boot in each hand dangling over his shoulder he carried me pick-a-back through the streets to the hospital, a large, fine building, formerly the "Balfour Hotel," and converted into a hospital after Portsmouth was captured. They took me up stairs into what was formerly the dining-room but now filled with over two hundred little iron beds, and each bed occupied by a wounded soldier. Everything in and about the place was as neat as wax. They carried me to a vacant bed near the centre of the room, and I noticed the next bed to mine had several tin dishes hanging over it, suspended from the ceiling. These were filled with water, and from a small hole punctured in the bottom the water would slowly but constantly drip upon some poor fellow's wound to keep it moist. I had just sat down on the side of my bed, when I was startled by the sound of a familiar voice. "Hello, cully! What you been doin', playing with one of those d—d shells, too?"

No, I replied, the shells were playing with me. Then I recognized the occupant of the next bed as my drummer boy acquaintance who had his hands blown off a week ago. What a strange thing that we should be brought together side by side again, both wounded with a shell and nearly on the same spot.

He had changed wonderfully; his little white pinched face told too plainly the suffering he had endured. I asked him how he was getting along.

"Oh I'm getting along pretty d—d fast. I guess I'll croak in a few days."

"Oh you mustn't talk that way, you'll be all right in a little while."

"Oh, no, cully, I know better. I'm a goner; I know it. I don't want to live, anyhow. What in h—l is the good of a man without hands?" Then turning his bandaged head towards me, his eyes filling with tears. "I ain't afraid to die, cul., but I would like to see my old mother first. Do you think I will?"

Oh, yes, I said, no doubt of it; at the same time I felt that his days were numbered, but I wanted to make him feel as comfortable as possible. He was so much worse off than I, that I forgot my own injuries and was eager to assist him all I could. After a few minutes silence—

"Say, cully, reach under my pillow and find a little book there; it's a little Testament that my dear old mother gave me; read a little for me, will you please? You'll find a place mother marked for me, read that, please."

I turned the leaves over till I found a little white ribbon pinned to a leaf, marking the verse beginning, "Suffer little children to come unto me." I started to read for him, but the tears filled my eyes. I had to stop, and as I did so, I noticed he seemed very quiet. I glanced at him, and the open, staring eyes and the rigid drawn features told me too plainly that the little fellow was out of his sufferings:—he was dead!

"Mother" was the countersign on his lips so thin, And the sentry in heaven _must_ let him in.

I remained here three weeks, finally got up and around and began to think I had enough of soldier life. I had everything I wished for; some ladies in the town—God bless them, I never will forget them—visited the hospital occasionally, and they always took pains to bring me flowers or goodies of some kind. (Pardon me, but somehow I was always a favourite with ladies.) Well, after remaining there three or four weeks I concluded I didn't want to go to the front, so I sat down and wrote a personal letter to Secretary Stanton, told him who, how, and what I was, and asked him to advise me what to do; if I should go to the front or home. Soon after, a special order came back from him to have me transferred to the "2nd Battalion Veteran Reserve Corps."

Let me here state to those who do not understand; all soldiers who were sick or wounded, unfit for field service were transferred to the Veteran Reserve Corps, for the purpose of doing light guard duty in camp, or at headquarters; they were divided into two battalions, 1st and 2nd. The 1st battalion was supposed to be able to carry a musket for duty, while the 2nd battalion was composed of one-armed men or totally disabled soldiers, and were supplied with a small sword; and thus I was condemned by special order; however I liked it. I had an easy time, nothing to do, and others to help me.

I continued here for about two months, until the hospital was ordered to be removed to Old Point Comfort. I had become a great favourite of Lieutenant Russell, the officer in charge of the hospital, and a nice man he was. When the order came to move, the fixtures, furniture, in fact everything in and about the building was ordered to be sold. I was detailed by Lieutenant Russell to remain behind and superintend the sale of the stuff, keep accounts, make a report when all was sold, and turn over the proceeds. That detained me there two weeks longer. I sold the beds, dishes, tables, everything. There remained about thirty tons of coal in the yard to be disposed of. I sold it in any quantity to poor people; took any price for it I could get, the same as everything else. Finally, everything was sold off, and I was ready to depart the next day for Old Point Comfort. In the evening, the two men I had with me and myself, used to get our pipes and sit in front of the office and smoke. We were sitting there talking about the sale, when it occurred to me that I had overlooked the "deadhouse." We went back to it and found seven coffins. What was to be done; they must be sold, as they must be accounted for, and we were going to depart early in the morning. The street was crowded at that time in the evening, so I took the coffins and stood them up on the sidewalk, and everyone that passed by, I would ask him if he wanted to buy a coffin. Finally, I struck a man who offered me seven dollars for the lot, and I took it quick. I learned afterward he was an undertaker.

The next day I landed and reported to headquarters at Fortress Monroe. A day or two after, Lieutenant Russell sent for me; he wanted a foreman in the Government Printing Office. I was down for occupation on the pay-roll as a printer. He asked me if I understood the business. I said yes, I had some knowledge of it, so I was detailed with an extra eight dollars per month. I took charge of the office at once. The first day I had orders to print fifty thousand official envelopes. The press-boy brought me the proof, I looked it over, and marked it correct; they were printed and sent to headquarters.

A few days after Lieutenant Russell sent for me to report at his office. I didn't know what was up. Thought perhaps I was going to be sent to Washington to take charge of the Government Printing Office there. As I went in, the lieutenant turned to me with a quizzical smile on his face:

"Young man, you told me you were a printer?"

"Yes, sir."

"Did you 'O. K.' this job?" passing one of the envelopes he held in his hand.

"Yes sir," I answered.

"Umph! Is it correct?"

"Yes, sir."

"It is, eh?"

"Yes–s, sir."

"Umph! how do you spell business?"

"B–u–i–s–n–e–ss," said I.

"You do, eh?"

"Yes, sir."

"Well," said he in an imperative manner, "our government sees fit to differ with you. You will go to your office and print fifty thousand more, but see that you spell business right, and bring me the proof. The lot you have printed we will send to Washington, and recommend that they be made into a *papier-mâché* statue of yourself, and label it 'Buisness' or the only government printer."

I was a little chagrined at the mistake, but did not take it to heart; but I was soon relieved by a man who was more careful in his spelling. A week or so after leaving the printing office, I was sent to the fort to act as a kind of a companion to the confederate president, Jefferson Davis. I was instructed to walk and talk with him. I presume I was intended for a sort of guard. Perhaps our government wished to make him feel as if he were not under surveillance, and so placed one whose insignificant appearance would put him at his ease. However, I found it a very agreeable occupation. One of the most pleasant weeks I ever passed was with Mr. Jefferson Davis. He was a most agreeable man to me. He gave me lots of good advice, and I learned more from conversation with him about national affairs than I ever expected to know; and if I ever become president I will avail myself of the advice and teaching of that great man. He pointed out the right and wrong paths for young men; urged me above all things to adhere strictly to honesty and integrity; to follow these two principles, and I would succeed in business and become great and respected. I thanked him for his kind advice, and pressed his hand good-bye. "Good-bye, my boy," said he. "You have been a comfort to me in my loneliness and sorrow. God bless you, my boy, God bless you!" A great, big something came up in my

FORTRESS MONROE WHERE JEFFERSON DAVIS WAS INCARCERATED

throat as I turned and left him, and I have regretted all my life that I was not fortunate enough to have the pleasure of meeting him again before he passed away; for I assure you, indulgent readers and comrades, that no matter what he had done, or what mistakes he had made, his memory will always find a warm spot in the heart of that little Drummer Boy from Maine.

One day, soon after this I sauntered down to the steamboat landing and was leisurely beguiling my time with a very large cigar. I noticed some commotion in the harbour but paid more attention to the cigar than anything else. Finally a large ocean steamer came in sight, rounded up near the wharf and let go her anchor. Very soon a "cutter" was lowered manned with sailors and pulled with steady stroke toward the wharf. While watching and wondering what they were going to do with the soldiers which I saw the vessel was loaded with, the "gig" or "cutter" neared the wharf, then I noticed particularly the young officer who sat in the stern, he was very dictatorial and pompous in his orders to the sailors, so much so that I said to myself, that fellow is putting on lots of airs; he thinks he's some pumpkins, I wish he'd fall overboard.

They finally reached the foot of the stairs, which led to the wharf. The young officer espied me and standing up in the boat shading his eyes with his hand seemed carefully contemplating me. I wondered if it could be possible that he had defined my wish and would have me arrested when he landed; perhaps it was the cigar that attracted his attention. It was against orders to smoke on the wharf, and such a big cigar in a boy's mouth looked very much out of place, but I wasn't going to give it up, and puffed more vigorously than ever. Just then the "cutter" touched the stairs that led up to the wharf with a bump, and the young officer with his handsome uniform turned a back-summersault overboard. It tickled me to death; I sat down and laughed to see him floundering to reach the stairs. I clapped my hands and cried, "Good, good!" He finally reached the stairs, clambered up onto them, but they being very slippery from the slime left by the ebbing tide, he lost his footing, his heels went into the air, and down again headfirst he went into the ocean.

I think he went clear to the bottom, for when he came up he was covered over with sea grass and mud. I laughed harder than before; everybody laughed, even the sailors, they couldn't help it, and when they fished him out he was a sight! The starch was out of his clothes, but not his pomposity. He roundly blamed the poor sailors. I sang out: "It wasn't their fault; what are you blaming them for?"

He looked at me and shook his fist. "Well, it wasn't!" and I thought to myself if I were they I would push him in again.

I then made up my mind I had better run, but I was so convulsed with laughter that I couldn't move. Hurriedly but cautiously climbing the slippery stairs, he made his way straight for me. I was still laughing, so hearty that my eyes were dimmed with tears! but I still puffed away at the big cigar. He looked at me for a moment, then hitting the cigar knocked it overboard, at the same time exclaiming, "You're too young to smoke. What you laughing at? Why don't you salute me? Discipline! I'll teach you discipline, confound you," at the same time boxing my ears. "You gorramed little cuss, why don't you salute me?" At the word *gorrame* I recovered myself, looked up and recognized my brother; he had been promoted since I saw him, had raised a full beard and was in command of a regiment on his way to New Orleans and had run into Fortress Monroe for orders and hoping to find me. I was more than pleased to see him, but wouldn't salute him until he had soundly cuffed my ears and threatened to throw me into the water.

When he was ready to depart he gave me a cigar and told me I could smoke it after he had gone, but I didn't; just as he was getting into the "cutter," I gave it to the Boatswain. I don't know, but I believe that cigar was loaded.

Soon after this episode, peace was declared, and the orders came to discharge all soldiers and send them to their respective homes, and on the 30th day of June, 1865, the boy who had worked so hard to get mustered into the service of Uncle Sam was discharged and mustered out. Then I went home to my dear, anxious family. I was not all covered with glory and I did not feel that I had saved my country, but was satisfied that I

A descriptive list belonging to Mr. Ulmer. The original is six times larger and was ploughed up with other documents by an old negro on the battle field in front of Petersburg, twelve years after the war. While Mr. Ulmer was playing an engagement at the theatre in Norfolk, the negro presented himself with the document all in pieces. Mr. Ulmer gave him $100 as a reward, had the pieces put together on parchment and it is now in a good state of preservation. The document is certainly a great relic; some portions of it are almost obliterated by mildew and exposure. The supposition is that the officer who had it in his possession was killed and the papers buried with him.

had not killed anyone; satisfied that I had furnished some little comfort and good cheer to my comrades during their hardships, and above all that I had learned the glorious distinction of being entitled to wear one of those little bronze buttons made from captured cannons and symbolic of the G. A. R.

Having spoken so often of my brother, some one may ask and wonder what became of him.

During the war our soldiers would often receive little useful articles, such as stockings, shirts, etc., made by the ladies who formed themselves into societies all over the country and furnished these things for distribution among the soldiers at the front. The young ladies had a great craze at that time of marking their names or initials upon whatever they made. One day my brother received a pair of hand-knit stockings with a little tag sewed on each of them, and written on the tags the letters L. A. D., Islesboro, Maine. They were so acceptable at the time that he declared that if he lived to get out of the army, he would be "gorramed" if he didn't find the girl that built those stockings, and kiss her for them. He began writing to Islesboro, making inquiries, and received several letters signed "Tab." He was determined not to give it up, however, and when mustered out, the first thing he did, was to go to Islesboro, Maine, to find "Tab." He found her, she was a schoolmarm, and soon after married her, and they are now living way out in Port Angeles in the State of Washington happy as bugs in a rug, and every meal time you can find several little "Tabs" around the table, some large enough to tell the story of how Pa found Ma, and a great desire to try the same thing themselves.

Epilogue

The unhappy war was over. The soldier boy returned. I arrived home at the little farm, found a royal, loving welcome from my father and brothers, and more than any other, my little step-sister, who never got tired of stories of my experience. She would sit for hours, begging me to tell her more. She was always with me wherever I would go. She was full of admiration for me. I was a hero in her eyes; I could not dispel her fancy, and I didn't try, for she seemed the sunshine of my life. She plodded with me through all my ups and downs; through the snow and ice of winter, making summer for me the year round, and she is now my little wife.

I must stop here, or I may go too far into a history of my life, which I did not intend. I know it would be uninteresting, but will simply add that myself and wife adopted the stage as a profession, and still follow it. I have just completed a play entitled, "The Volunteer" which I shall soon submit for public approval.

* * * * *

My recollections are finished—for they are but recollections of a time that "tried men's souls." In looking back o'er the path of life there is a melancholy pleasure, to me, at least, in contemplating the shattered shards of many an air built castle,—inhaling the perfumes of flowers long since faded and dead. If these reflections have served to beguile one moment of "ennui" for an idle reader—if they have recalled one incident of "derring do" to a whilesome comrade, I am satisfied that my purpose is accomplished.

LEONAUR

ALSO FROM LEONAUR
AVAILABLE IN SOFTCOVER OR HARDCOVER WITH DUST JACKET

A HISTORY OF THE FRENCH & INDIAN WAR *by Arthur G. Bradley*—The Seven Years War as it was fought in the New World has always fascinated students of military history—here is the story of that confrontation.

WASHINGTON'S EARLY CAMPAIGNS *by James Hadden*—The French Post Expedition, Great Meadows and Braddock's Defeat—including Braddock's Orderly Books.

BOUQUET & THE OHIO INDIAN WAR *by Cyrus Cort & William Smith*—Two Accounts of the Campaigns of 1763-1764: Bouquet's Campaigns by Cyrus Cort & The History of Bouquet's Expeditions by William Smith.

NARRATIVES OF THE FRENCH & INDIAN WAR: 2 *by David Holden, Samuel Jenks, Lemuel Lyon, Mary Cochrane Rogers & Henry T. Blake*—Contains The Diary of Sergeant David Holden, Captain Samuel Jenks' Journal, The Journal of Lemuel Lyon, Journal of a French Officer at the Siege of Quebec, A Battle Fought on Snowshoes & The Battle of Lake George.

NARRATIVES OF THE FRENCH & INDIAN WAR *by Brown, Eastburn, Hawks & Putnam*—Ranger Brown's Narrative, The Adventures of Robert Eastburn, The Journal of Rufus Putnam—Provincial Infantry & Orderly Book and Journal of Major John Hawks on the Ticonderoga-Crown Point Campaign.

THE 7TH (QUEEN'S OWN) HUSSARS: Volume 1—1688-1792 *by C. R. B. Barrett*—As Dragoons During the Flanders Campaign, War of the Austrian Succession and the Seven Years War.

INDIA'S FREE LANCES *by H. G. Keene*—European Mercenary Commanders in Hindustan 1770-1820.

THE BENGAL EUROPEAN REGIMENT *by P. R. Innes*—An Elite Regiment of the Honourable East India Company 1756-1858.

MUSKET & TOMAHAWK *by Francis Parkman*—A Military History of the French & Indian War, 1753-1760.

THE BLACK WATCH AT TICONDEROGA *by Frederick B. Richards*—Campaigns in the French & Indian War.

QUEEN'S RANGERS *by Frederick B. Richards*—John Simcoe and his Rangers During the Revolutionary War for America.

LEONAUR

ALSO FROM LEONAUR
AVAILABLE IN SOFTCOVER OR HARDCOVER WITH DUST JACKET

OFFICERS & GENTLEMEN *by Peter Hawker & William Graham*—Two Accounts of British Officers During the Peninsula War: Officer of Light Dragoons by Peter Hawker & Campaign in Portugal and Spain by William Graham .

THE WALCHEREN EXPEDITION *by Anonymous*—The Experiences of a British Officer of the 81st Regt. During the Campaign in the Low Countries of 1809.

LADIES OF WATERLOO *by Charlotte A. Eaton, Magdalene de Lancey & Juana Smith*—The Experiences of Three Women During the Campaign of 1815: Waterloo Days by Charlotte A. Eaton, A Week at Waterloo by Magdalene de Lancey & Juana's Story by Juana Smith.

JOURNAL OF AN OFFICER IN THE KING'S GERMAN LEGION *by John Frederick Hering*—Recollections of Campaigning During the Napoleonic Wars.

JOURNAL OF AN ARMY SURGEON IN THE PENINSULAR WAR *by Charles Boutflower*—The Recollections of a British Army Medical Man on Campaign During the Napoleonic Wars.

ON CAMPAIGN WITH MOORE AND WELLINGTON *by Anthony Hamilton*—The Experiences of a Soldier of the 43rd Regiment During the Peninsular War.

THE ROAD TO AUSTERLITZ *by R. G. Burton*—Napoleon's Campaign of 1805.

SOLDIERS OF NAPOLEON *by A. J. Doisy De Villargennes & Arthur Chuquet*—The Experiences of the Men of the French First Empire: Under the Eagles by A. J. Doisy De Villargennes & Voices of 1812 by Arthur Chuquet .

INVASION OF FRANCE, 1814 *by F. W. O. Maycock*—The Final Battles of the Napoleonic First Empire.

LEIPZIG—A CONFLICT OF TITANS *by Frederic Shoberl*—A Personal Experience of the 'Battle of the Nations' During the Napoleonic Wars, October 14th-19th, 1813.

SLASHERS *by Charles Cadell*—The Campaigns of the 28th Regiment of Foot During the Napoleonic Wars by a Serving Officer.

BATTLE IMPERIAL *by Charles William Vane*—The Campaigns in Germany & France for the Defeat of Napoleon 1813-1814.

SWIFT & BOLD *by Gibbes Rigaud*—The 60th Rifles During the Peninsula War.

ALSO FROM LEONAUR
AVAILABLE IN SOFTCOVER OR HARDCOVER WITH DUST JACKET

COLBORNE: A SINGULAR TALENT FOR WAR *by John Colborne*—The Napoleonic Wars Career of One of Wellington's Most Highly Valued Officers in Egypt, Holland, Italy, the Peninsula and at Waterloo.

NAPOLEON'S RUSSIAN CAMPAIGN *by Philippe Henri de Segur*—The Invasion, Battles and Retreat by an Aide-de-Camp on the Emperor's Staff.

WITH THE LIGHT DIVISION *by John H. Cooke*—The Experiences of an Officer of the 43rd Light Infantry in the Peninsula and South of France During the Napoleonic Wars.

WELLINGTON AND THE PYRENEES CAMPAIGN VOLUME I: FROM VITORIA TO THE BIDASSOA *by F. C. Beatson*—The final phase of the campaign in the Iberian Peninsula.

WELLINGTON AND THE INVASION OF FRANCE VOLUME II: THE BIDASSOA TO THE BATTLE OF THE NIVELLE *by F. C. Beatson*—The final phase of the campaign in the Iberian Peninsula.

WELLINGTON AND THE FALL OF FRANCE VOLUME III: THE GAVES AND THE BATTLE OF ORTHEZ *by F. C. Beatson*—The final phase of the campaign in the Iberian Peninsula.

NAPOLEON'S IMPERIAL GUARD: FROM MARENGO TO WATERLOO *by J. T. Headley*—The story of Napoleon's Imperial Guard and the men who commanded them.

BATTLES & SIEGES OF THE PENINSULAR WAR *by W. H. Fitchett*—Corunna, Busaco, Albuera, Ciudad Rodrigo, Badajos, Salamanca, San Sebastian & Others.

SERGEANT GUILLEMARD: THE MAN WHO SHOT NELSON? *by Robert Guillemard*—A Soldier of the Infantry of the French Army of Napoleon on Campaign Throughout Europe.

WITH THE GUARDS ACROSS THE PYRENEES *by Robert Batty*—The Experiences of a British Officer of Wellington's Army During the Battles for the Fall of Napoleonic France, 1813 .

A STAFF OFFICER IN THE PENINSULA *by E. W. Buckham*—An Officer of the British Staff Corps Cavalry During the Peninsula Campaign of the Napoleonic Wars.

THE LEIPZIG CAMPAIGN: 1813—NAPOLEON AND THE "BATTLE OF THE NATIONS" *by F. N. Maude*—Colonel Maude's analysis of Napoleon's campaign of 1813 around Leipzig.

LEONAUR

ALSO FROM LEONAUR
AVAILABLE IN SOFTCOVER OR HARDCOVER WITH DUST JACKET

BUGEAUD: A PACK WITH A BATON *by Thomas Robert Bugeaud*—The Early Campaigns of a Soldier of Napoleon's Army Who Would Become a Marshal of France.

WATERLOO RECOLLECTIONS *by Frederick Llewellyn*—Rare First Hand Accounts, Letters, Reports and Retellings from the Campaign of 1815.

SERGEANT NICOL *by Daniel Nicol*—The Experiences of a Gordon Highlander During the Napoleonic Wars in Egypt, the Peninsula and France.

THE JENA CAMPAIGN: 1806 *by F. N. Maude*—The Twin Battles of Jena & Auerstadt Between Napoleon's French and the Prussian Army.

PRIVATE O'NEIL *by Charles O'Neil*—The recollections of an Irish Rogue of H. M. 28th Regt.—The Slashers—during the Peninsula & Waterloo campaigns of the Napoleonic war.

ROYAL HIGHLANDER *by James Anton*—A soldier of H.M 42nd (Royal) Highlanders during the Peninsular, South of France & Waterloo Campaigns of the Napoleonic Wars.

CAPTAIN BLAZE *by Elzéar Blaze*—Life in Napoleons Army.

LEJEUNE VOLUME 1 *by Louis-François Lejeune*—The Napoleonic Wars through the Experiences of an Officer on Berthier's Staff.

LEJEUNE VOLUME 2 *by Louis-François Lejeune*—The Napoleonic Wars through the Experiences of an Officer on Berthier's Staff.

CAPTAIN COIGNET *by Jean-Roch Coignet*—A Soldier of Napoleon's Imperial Guard from the Italian Campaign to Russia and Waterloo.

FUSILIER COOPER *by John S. Cooper*—Experiences in the 7th (Royal) Fusiliers During the Peninsular Campaign of the Napoleonic Wars and the American Campaign to New Orleans.

FIGHTING NAPOLEON'S EMPIRE *by Joseph Anderson*—The Campaigns of a British Infantryman in Italy, Egypt, the Peninsular & the West Indies During the Napoleonic Wars.

CHASSEUR BARRES *by Jean-Baptiste Barres*—The experiences of a French Infantryman of the Imperial Guard at Austerlitz, Jena, Eylau, Friedland, in the Peninsular, Lutzen, Bautzen, Zinnwald and Hanau during the Napoleonic Wars.

![LEONAUR logo]

ALSO FROM LEONAUR
AVAILABLE IN SOFTCOVER OR HARDCOVER WITH DUST JACKET

THE RELUCTANT REBEL *by William G. Stevenson*—A young Kentuckian's experiences in the Confederate Infantry & Cavalry during the American Civil War..

BOOTS AND SADDLES *by Elizabeth B. Custer*—The experiences of General Custer's Wife on the Western Plains.

FANNIE BEERS' CIVIL WAR *by Fannie A. Beers*—A Confederate Lady's Experiences of Nursing During the Campaigns & Battles of the American Civil War.

LADY SALE'S AFGHANISTAN *by Florentia Sale*—An Indomitable Victorian Lady's Account of the Retreat from Kabul During the First Afghan War.

THE TWO WARS OF MRS DUBERLY *by Frances Isabella Duberly*—An Intrepid Victorian Lady's Experience of the Crimea and Indian Mutiny.

THE REBELLIOUS DUCHESS *by Paul F. S. Dermoncourt*—The Adventures of the Duchess of Berri and Her Attempt to Overthrow French Monarchy.

LADIES OF WATERLOO *by Charlotte A. Eaton, Magdalene de Lancey & Juana Smith*—The Experiences of Three Women During the Campaign of 1815: Waterloo Days by Charlotte A. Eaton, A Week at Waterloo by Magdalene de Lancey & Juana's Story by Juana Smith.

TWO YEARS BEFORE THE MAST *by Richard Henry Dana. Jr.*—The account of one young man's experiences serving on board a sailing brig—the Penelope—bound for California, between the years 1834-36.

A SAILOR OF KING GEORGE *by Frederick Hoffman*—From Midshipman to Captain—Recollections of War at Sea in the Napoleonic Age 1793-1815.

LORDS OF THE SEA *by A. T. Mahan*—Great Captains of the Royal Navy During the Age of Sail.

COGGESHALL'S VOYAGES: VOLUME 1 *by George Coggeshall*—The Recollections of an American Schooner Captain.

COGGESHALL'S VOYAGES: VOLUME 2 *by George Coggeshall*—The Recollections of an American Schooner Captain.

TWILIGHT OF EMPIRE *by Sir Thomas Ussher & Sir George Cockburn*—Two accounts of Napoleon's Journeys in Exile to Elba and St. Helena: Narrative of Events by Sir Thomas Ussher & Napoleon's Last Voyage: Extract of a diary by Sir George Cockburn.

LEONAUR

ALSO FROM LEONAUR

AVAILABLE IN SOFTCOVER OR HARDCOVER WITH DUST JACKET

IRON TIMES WITH THE GUARDS *by An O. E. (G. P. A. Fildes)*—The Experiences of an Officer of the Coldstream Guards on the Western Front During the First World War.

THE GREAT WAR IN THE MIDDLE EAST: 1 *by W. T. Massey*—The Desert Campaigns & How Jerusalem Was Won---two classic accounts in one volume.

THE GREAT WAR IN THE MIDDLE EAST: 2 *by W. T. Massey*—Allenby's Final Triumph.

SMITH-DORRIEN *by Horace Smith-Dorrien*—Isandlwhana to the Great War.

1914 *by Sir John French*—The Early Campaigns of the Great War by the British Commander.

GRENADIER *by E. R. M. Fryer*—The Recollections of an Officer of the Grenadier Guards throughout the Great War on the Western Front.

BATTLE, CAPTURE & ESCAPE *by George Pearson*—The Experiences of a Canadian Light Infantryman During the Great War.

DIGGERS AT WAR *by R. Hugh Knyvett & G. P. Cuttriss*—"Over There" With the Australians by R. Hugh Knyvett and Over the Top With the Third Australian Division by G. P. Cuttriss. Accounts of Australians During the Great War in the Middle East, at Gallipoli and on the Western Front.

HEAVY FIGHTING BEFORE US *by George Brenton Laurie*—The Letters of an Officer of the Royal Irish Rifles on the Western Front During the Great War.

THE CAMELIERS *by Oliver Hogue*—A Classic Account of the Australians of the Imperial Camel Corps During the First World War in the Middle East.

RED DUST *by Donald Black*—A Classic Account of Australian Light Horsemen in Palestine During the First World War.

THE LEAN, BROWN MEN *by Angus Buchanan*—Experiences in East Africa During the Great War with the 25th Royal Fusiliers—the Legion of Frontiersmen.

THE NIGERIAN REGIMENT IN EAST AFRICA *by W. D. Downes*—On Campaign During the Great War 1916-1918.

THE 'DIE-HARDS' IN SIBERIA *by John Ward*—With the Middlesex Regiment Against the Bolsheviks 1918-19.

ALSO FROM LEONAUR

AVAILABLE IN SOFTCOVER OR HARDCOVER WITH DUST JACKET

FARAWAY CAMPAIGN *by F. James*—Experiences of an Indian Army Cavalry Officer in Persia & Russia During the Great War.

REVOLT IN THE DESERT *by T. E. Lawrence*—An account of the experiences of one remarkable British officer's war from his own perspective.

MACHINE-GUN SQUADRON *by A. M. G.*—The 20th Machine Gunners from British Yeomanry Regiments in the Middle East Campaign of the First World War.

A GUNNER'S CRUSADE *by Antony Bluett*—The Campaign in the Desert, Palestine & Syria as Experienced by the Honourable Artillery Company During the Great War .

DESPATCH RIDER *by W. H. L. Watson*—The Experiences of a British Army Motorcycle Despatch Rider During the Opening Battles of the Great War in Europe.

TIGERS ALONG THE TIGRIS *by E. J. Thompson*—The Leicestershire Regiment in Mesopotamia During the First World War.

HEARTS & DRAGONS *by Charles R. M. F. Crutwell*—The 4th Royal Berkshire Regiment in France and Italy During the Great War, 1914-1918.

INFANTRY BRIGADE: 1914 *by John Ward*—The Diary of a Commander of the 15th Infantry Brigade, 5th Division, British Army, During the Retreat from Mons.

DOING OUR 'BIT' *by Ian Hay*—Two Classic Accounts of the Men of Kitchener's 'New Army' During the Great War including *The First 100,000* & *All In It*.

AN EYE IN THE STORM *by Arthur Ruhl*—An American War Correspondent's Experiences of the First World War from the Western Front to Gallipoli-and Beyond.

STAND & FALL *by Joe Cassells*—With the Middlesex Regiment Against the Bolsheviks 1918-19.

RIFLEMAN MACGILL'S WAR *by Patrick MacGill*—A Soldier of the London Irish During the Great War in Europe including *The Amateur Army*, *The Red Horizon* & *The Great Push*.

WITH THE GUNS *by C. A. Rose & Hugh Dalton*—Two First Hand Accounts of British Gunners at War in Europe During World War 1- Three Years in France with the Guns and With the British Guns in Italy.

THE BUSH WAR DOCTOR *by Robert V. Dolbey*—The Experiences of a British Army Doctor During the East African Campaign of the First World War.